Just Do This Stuff

Just Do This Stuff

The Practical Application of Success

LARRY WINGET

Just Do This Stuff

By
Larry Winget

Published by:
Win Publications!
A subsidiary of Win Seminars!, Inc.
Tulsa, Oklahoma – Scottsdale, Arizona
www.larrywinget.com
800 749-4597

Printed in the United States of America.

Cover design and layout by Ad Graphics, Inc., Tulsa, OK

Library of Congress Catalog Number: 95-060072

ISBN: 1-881342-28-X

10 9 8 7 6 5 4 3 2 1

Also by Larry Winget

That Makes Me Sick!
The Simple Way To Success
Money Is Easy
Stuff That Works Every Single Day
The Little Red Book Of Stuff That Works
Profound Stuff
Success One Day At A Time
Just So This Stuff
How To Write A Book One Page At A Time
The Wit And Wisdom Of Larry Winget

Anthologies:
Only The Best On Success
Only The Best On Leadership
Only The Best On Customer Service
Outlaw Wisdom
The Outlaws Of Success

Dedication

I dedicate this book to the doers of the world.

To all those who take responsibility,
make no excuses,
and figure out a way to get it done . . .
regardless!

Contents

Introduction

I read over one hundred books a year on the subjects of leadership, selling, customer service, business, money, philosophy, religion, spirituality, humor, psychology, self-help, motivation, and more! These books have shaped me and my thinking more than I can even begin to explain. Few things give me more pleasure than finding a great book and delving into the new ideas it has to offer me.

However . . .

One evening, as I reached for another book on my to-be-read shelf, I realized that most books are only *about* things and very few offer practical steps on how to really get these things done. In fact, as I perused the dozen books that I had written, I realized that most of what I had written was information and opinions *about* things. It's not that books about things aren't good. In fact, I think that books about things are terrific. It's just that every once in a while, you ought to be able to pick up a book full of lists of just-do-this-stuff-and-you-will-get-things-done information. Major problem – very few books with lists like that exist.

Until now.

Before You Begin

The stuff you are about to read is simple stuff. Profoundly simple. Amazingly simple. In fact, it's so simple that most people will never do it.

Let me give you two quotes that sum it up very well:

Success does not come from doing extraordinary things.

Success comes from doing ordinary things, extraordinarily well.

... Unknown

What is easy to do is also easy not to do.

... Jim Rohn

So don't pass these steps by too quickly. Yes, they are simple. But those of you who decide to do them will be happy, successful, healthy, and rich!

One more time.

This stuff is not rocket science! It's just not that tough to live a life of health, happiness, success, and prosperity.

So . . .

read the lists, **do** the lists, and **enjoy** the rewards!

Every list begins with these two steps.

1. **Decide.**
   If you want to do something, then just decide to do it. If you want to be something, then decide to be it. If you want to have something, then decide to have it.

   You are what you are, do what you do, and have what you have, all because you decided it. If you had decided something different, then your experience would have been different.

2. **Believe.**
   If you want to be more, do more, and have more, then believe that it's possible. Your belief will manifest itself in your actions and then in your results. The stronger your belief, the faster the results.

When you mess up...
BIG DEAL!
Just admit it, fix it and move on.
other than that,
life is a party!
©Larry Winget, 800 749-4597

To Take Responsibility

just do this stuff:

1. Understand that taking responsibility is the most critical step you will make in becoming successful at anything you undertake. Taking responsibility for everything you are, everything you do, and everything you have, is the hardest thing you will ever accomplish. However, it will do you no good to go any further until you have done it. You cannot skip this step.

2. Make a list of all the things that are keeping you from being as successful as you would like to be.

3. Make sure that your name is on the list.

4. Throw the list away.

5. Stop blaming others regardless of how you feel they may have wronged you.

6. Move on!

To Enjoy Life More

just do this stuff:

1. Lighten up!
2. Forget blame.
3. Forget guilt.
4. Forget luck.
5. Make your own circumstances.
6. Focus on the present.

7. Look for the good.

8. Expect the best.

9. Be prepared for the worst.

10. Celebrate it all!

To Set And Achieve Goals

just do this stuff:

1. Remember the Rules Of Goal Setting:

Write your goals down.

Make your goals big.

Make some of your goals small.

Make your goals very specific.

Make sure that the goals you work on are really yours.

Make sure that your goals are not in conflict with each other.

State your goal as an affirmation.

2. Make three lists.

   The first, "Everything You Want To Be;" the second, "Everything You Want To Do;" the third, "Everything You Want To Have."

3. Pick one of the things on the list to work on.

4. Write down exactly why you want it. Make this really good.

5. Write down the obstacles you will face in achieving your goal. (This is not a place for whining. Only list legitimate obstacles.)

6. Write down everything you already know about how to achieve your goal.

7. Write down everything you need to know in order to achieve your goal.

8. Write down the names of the people who can help you achieve your goal.

9. Write down a plan on how you will achieve your goal.

10. Write down something that you can do today to get started.

11. Determine a completion date for achieving your goal.

12. Figure out how you will celebrate achieving your goal.

13. Repeat the process for each of your goals.

14. Visualize success.

15. Suspend disbelief. You can do it if you believe you can!

Expect The Best.
Be Prepared
For The
Worst.
Celebrate It All!
Larry Winget

To Make More Money

just do this stuff:

1. Believe that you deserve more money.

2. Do more than you are paid to do. Soon you will be paid more for what you do.

3. Make a list of all the ways you can add value to the lives of others: your customers; your boss; your family; your friends; strangers.

4. Become a problem solver. Your ability to solve problems will determine your income.

5. Believe in what you do, the company you do it for, your customers, and in yourself.

6. Love what you do and the money will come.

7. Visualize more money.

8. Be thankful for the money you already have.

9. Study prosperity. Buy good books on investing, saving, money management, prosperity, and how to serve others.

10. Give away some of your money on a regular basis.

11. Save something.

12. Spend wisely and happily.

To Be Better Read

just do this stuff:

While there are many amazing books out there, books that can and will really change your life (and you should do your best to read every one of them) these are a handful of my favorites that I just can't imagine going through life without having read.

Non-fiction

Beachcombing At Miramar By Richard Bode

The Seven Spiritual Laws Of Success By Deepak Chopra

Unconditional Life By Deepak Chopra

The Richest Man In Babylon By George S. Clason

Real Magic By Wayne Dyer

Wisdom Of The Ages By Wayne Dyer

How To Get Your Point Across IN 30 Seconds Or Less By Milo Frank

You Can Heal Your Life By Louise Hay

The Ultimate Secret To Getting Absolutely Everything You Want By Mike Hernacki

The Science Of Mind By Ernest Holmes

The Greatest Salesman In The World By Og Mandino

Bringing Out The Best In People By Alan Loy McGinnis

Mutant Message Down Under By Marlo Morgan

You Can Have It All By Arnold Patent

You Were Born Rich By Bob Proctor

Seven Strategies For Wealth And Happiness By James Rohn

The Magic Of Thinking Big By David Schwartz

You Are The Power By Kennedy J. Shultz

Conversations With God, Book One By Neale Donald Walsh

Conversations With God, Book Two By Neale Donald Walsh

Conversations With God, Book Three By Neale Donald Walsh

Friendship With God By Neale Donald Walsh

Enchanted Love By Marianne Williamson

A Return To Love By Marianne Williamson

Money Is Easy By Larry H. Winget

The Law Of Success By Paramahansa Yogananda

Fiction

There are just too many to mention here. I choose the fiction books I read based on my mood, the location I am going to read them, the time I have available and many other reasons. I read about 50 fiction books a year. Therefore I just can't recommend a list because there would be far too many. But of all the fiction books I recommend every time to every person this is the one book I insist you read:

A Prayer For Owen Meany By John Irving

To Be A Better Parent

just do this stuff:

1. Kids are NOT little adults. Don't treat them like they are.

2. Be consistent.

3. Make the punishment fit the crime.

4. When your teenager's room is a mess, shut the door. Save both of you the frustration. By the time they are teenagers it's too late.

5. Cut them some slack from time to time. After all, they're kids.

6. Don't cut them too much slack. You do your children a great disservice by being too lenient or by being inconsistent.

7. If you have little bitty kids, sit on the floor a lot. Physically communicate at their level.

8. Don't expect perfection. Especially when it comes to grades. Ask them to do their best, regardless of what that might be and then be satisfied with that. And teach them to be satisfied with their best as well.

9. Teach them the really important things: kindness, charity, love, forgiveness, compassion, respect, honesty, how to take responsibility and how to have fun.

10. Teach them about money. How to earn it, save it, invest it and spend it.

11. Play with your kids at every opportunity.

12. Listen to them.

13. Ask more, tell less.

14. Hug more, nag less.

15. Show your kids affection even after they think they are too big for it.

16. Respect your child's privacy.

17. Encourage your children to develop their own uniqueness. Don't try to mold their personalities. Let them be who they are and NOT who you want them to be.

18. Don't make a jackass out of yourself at their sporting events. Too big of a fan is embarrassing to them, to yourself and to all of those watching you. Which means don't be obnoxious to the other team, or to the coaches, or other parents, or officials.

19. Respect them enough to tell them the truth.

20. Know your kid's friends. And have them over to your house. Better to have a house full of rowdy kids than to wonder where your child is.

Larry's Two Golden Rules Of Parenting

Remember:
They grow out of it.
They need love more than stuff.

To Be More Giving

just do this stuff:

1. Pick a worthy cause.

2. Commit to giving ten percent of your income to the worthy cause.

3. Give every time you receive money.

4. Be thankful that you have the ability to give.

5. Remember that giving is a physical principle as much as it is a spiritual principle. Giving causes a vacuum that will be filled by the Universe. Trust the principle.

6. Give more than your money. Give your time; your love; or a smile. Give anything and everything that you have.

7. Give what you lack. That way you are assured of receiving what you need.

8. Make giving a habit.

9. Give cheerfully.

To Lose Weight

just do this stuff:

1. Stop going to fast food restaurants as often. They make their living with grease. They have to use grease to cover up the fact that they aren't serving you any real food. Now don't kid yourself, grease tastes good. I like it. And it's okay every once in a while but you can't do it every day. And don't use convenience or price as an excuse; those places are rarely that fast and they certainly aren't economical.

2. Eat high fiber foods. Get regular and surprise yourself on the scales. To help, buy some Dieter's Tea at the health food store. This is best way to stay "cleansed" that I have discovered.

3. Don't take pills to lose weight. You didn't get fat taking pills and you aren't going to get skinny taking pills either. (However, this is really one that you should discuss with your *skinny* doctor. Sometimes medication is required – but that over-the-counter stuff won't help you lose weight long term.)

4. Leave the parking spaces close to the door for the old people and the wimps. You need to walk. Park as far away as you can without having to cross a major thoroughfare on foot. (Fat folks don't run across streets well and they make excellent targets.)

5. Take a friend, your dog, your kid, or your spousal unit for a walk – even if it is only around the block. It is good for your body and promotes conversation – thus making it also good for your relationship (even with your dog).

6. Don't get on the scales very often. In fact, about every two weeks is more than enough. If you weigh every day you will only get discouraged – weight doesn't come off every day. Give it some time.

7. When you lose some weight, go buy something new to wear. You will feel like a million bucks and be proud of your accomplishments.

8. When you lose a little more weight, go to the tailor and have your clothes taken in. It will make you feel so proud of yourself to actually have things taken in instead of let out like you have been doing. If your clothes are not worth altering, then give them away or throw them away. Do not keep them around "just in case" you gain it back. Don't make plans to get fat again. Don't leave yourself an excuse to retreat to fatdom.

9. Don't think fat, don't think fit, in fact, don't think. If you focus on your weight, it will become an obsession and make you hungry or make you have angst about what you could have done or should be doing. Simply do what you know is right. Period.

10. Don't beat yourself up for slipping. If you are absolutely going crazy for a pizza, then eat it. And enjoy it completely. Then adjust tomorrow.

11. When you splurge, do it in front of a toilet or wastebasket. (I said splurge, not purge!) This is just a trick I learned. When I want something, like a bag of M&M's, then I buy a bag of M&M's. I open it in front of the toilet or a trash can and after eating a few – just enough to get the taste (which is all I really wanted in the first place) I throw them away. Suggestion: Use a public trash can so you won't dive in for them later. See why a toilet is preferable?

12. Find a buddy to go eat with. And not a person who will tempt you with fattening food or take you to places you know you shouldn't be.

13. When you are hungry, stay away from places that serve food. Places like the mall (food courts) and the grocery store. If you need to go out and you know it is to a place where you will be tempted, then drink a huge glass of water before you go to fill yourself up.

14. Willpower is overestimated. It is hard to come by and impossible to count on so don't. The best thing you can do is to just keep yourself away from situations where you might disappoint yourself.

15. When you stop for gasoline go to a "pay at the pump" station. That way you won't be tempted to buy a soda or candy bar when you go in to pay.

16. Drink lots of water. Gallons of it. Carry a bottle of it with you all the time. It will fill you up and keep you running to the bathroom, which burns calories.

17. Stop lying to yourself and everyone else. You don't have a glandular problem. The percentage of people in the world who actually have one is so small that they don't even count. And you arc NOT "big boned." Your frame may be larger than others but your bones are not the problem; the fat you pack on those bones is the problem. And don't say "My family is heavy, we are just heavy people." That is no excuse. Chances are it isn't hereditary. And being fat does NOT "run" in your family. In fact, I'll bet no one "runs" in your family. The reason your family is fat is that they eat like pigs. Period. And you grew up thinking that was normal. You probably think everyone puts gravy on cereal. So it isn't in

your genes. You probably haven't been able to fit in your jeans for a good long while.

18. Eat cereal. Not Count Chocula or Trix (remember, Trix are for kids – fat hyperactive kids). Eat high fiber stuff like Shredded Wheat, Raisin Bran, Grape Nuts, Chex – stuff like that. Eat it all the time for all meals. Eat a small bowl of it before you go out to dinner to fill you up. Eat it for dessert instead of a Ding-Dong. It is full of vitamins and it is relatively low in calories and fat compared to most other foods and it will keep you regular. Hint: don't cover it with whole milk, half-and-half, cream or gravy; stick with skim milk, 1% or 2%.

19. Do something. I am not saying exercise but you can call it that if you want to. I am just saying do something. Turn the TV off and get off your fat butt and go for a walk. You don't need a gym. You need to walk or ride a bicycle or have sex – anything that makes your heart beat a little harder. So do something aerobic and combine it with muscle

training. And make it fun. If you don't enjoy it, you won't stick with it.

20. The short list for weighing less: eat less.

And what I believe to be the biggy; the one they NEVER tell you about in the diet books:

Never deprive yourself of anything.

Eat whatever you want – just not much of it and not very often.

Success is simple,
Money is easy,
Life is a HOOT!
©Larry Winget, 800 749-4597

To Have More Fun

just do this stuff:

1. Lighten up!
2. Do something several times per day that makes you laugh.
3. Read humor books.
4. Listen to humor tapes.
5. Make a list of things that you consider to be fun.

6. Work the things on your Fun list into your schedule on a regular basis.

7. Set aside a portion of your income (after you have given some, saved some, and paid your obligations) for having fun.

8. Buy yourself a toy. Try a yo-yo, slinky, or jacks.

9. Own a whoopee cushion and red socks.

10. Ask little kids how to have fun . . . they know!

To Be A Better Spouse

just do this stuff:

1. Make a list of everything you like about your spouse. Be very specific.

2. Commit to telling your spouse one of the things on the list every day.

3. Make another list. This one should describe the kind of spouse you would like to have.

4. Become the person on this list.

5. Leave your spouse little notes telling them how much you love them.
6. Laugh together often.
7. Go more than half way. Go more than all the way. Go as far as it takes and then some.
8. Become a better listener.
9. Hug more. Gripe less.
10. Scope up. Never be petty.
11. Treat your spouse with the same dignity and respect that you would a stranger.
12. Look good for your spouse.

To Dress Better

just do this stuff:

"If you are going to bother being dressed, be well dressed."

. . . Dale Irvin

Fashion Tips For Everyone:

1. Be careful what you wear in public. Trust me – you will be seen in it. Think about how you would feel bumping into your best customer before you run out the door in the pair of sweats with the baggy butt and the hole in the knee.

2. Go easy on the perfume or cologne. I shouldn't smell you from across the room.

Perfume is like Brylcream; a little dab will do ya.

3. If you don't think you know what is in style because it changes so fast, then watch some television and buy some magazines.

4. Trendy is one thing. I like trends. But to become their slave is silly and expensive and makes you look like a person without style rather than a person of style.

5. Belly bags/fanny packs . . . don't. Really. Please. Just don't.

6. If you travel out of the United States and want to make sure you look like a tourist, then be sure to wear blue jeans. Then if you want to look like a goobery tourist, put on a fanny pack and athletic shoes. This is a guaranteed way to spot a tourist.

"Style is being yourself on purpose."
. . . Raquel Welch

"How you look tells the world how you feel."
. . . Sergio Valente

7. Black always works. From head to toe. It makes you look richer, classier, and best of all: you will look slimmer. (By the way, women have known this for years and never shared this helpful little bit of information. They never told us if we put it in black it would look smaller. That's why I don't have any black underwear.)

Fashion Tips For Men.

1. Ties should be tied so that the end of the tie, preferably the big end, hits at the bottom of the belt. If you are tall or extremely long waisted or have a fat gut then buy your ties at the Big and Tall Store so they will be long enough.

2. Ties should not advertise your favorite team or be covered with bottles of hot sauce, cartoon characters or dead rock musicians.

3. The above statement also applies to socks.

4. It is never acceptable to loosen your tie, except when you are taking it off.

"If men can run the world, why can't they stop wearing neckties? How intelligent is it to start the day by tying a little noose around your neck?"

. . . Linda Ellerbee

5. Shoes should be shined. Always. They should also match your belt. Always. Loafers never go with a suit. Penny loafers don't really go with anything, Fonzie. They are history. And in my personal opinion so are tassel loafers unless you really want everyone to consider you a pretentious goober.

6. Pants should hit your shoes. Not so long that you walk on them, but long enough to break (bend at the shoe). If I can see your socks while you are standing then your pants are too short.

7. Be careful with knit shirts. If they are too tight then you will look fat. For the most part: if the knit stretches, the shirt is too tight. However, if your chest really is bigger than your gut then you might be able to pull it off. Otherwise forget it.

8. About dress shirts. They DO NOT come in short sleeves. Button down shirts are NOT dress shirts; they are casual shirts and should not be worn with a suit. However, they may be worn with khaki pants and a sport coat.

9. Never wear Bike shorts unless you are really a coach. (I am not talking about Bicycle shorts; you guys know what I mean. They are those double knit shorts that have a button waist made to be worn without a belt and are often seen on overweight aging jocks.)

Fashion Tips For Women.

1. Don't tie a coat or sweater around your waist. If you aren't a size two or smaller then you are going to look like you have a huge butt.

2. Don't wear white hose unless you work in a hospital and they absolutely force you. White hose make you look like your legs are heavy.

3. Remember this: Just because it looks good on Cindy Crawford, that doesn't mean it is going to look good on you.

4. Sales people lie. It is their job to say, "That looks darling on you!"

5. No Christmas sweaters (or Halloween sweaters or Easter sweaters or Thanksgiving sweaters or any other holiday where anything can be woven into or embroidered on a sweater).

6. Shoes make the outfit. Shoes can take a blah outfit and make it dazzling. And while high heels may be uncomfortable and even bad for you, remember men are pigs and we love them.

7. For the most part, hats make you look stupid. There are exceptions I guess, maybe on Easter or a ball cap with a ponytail pulled through it but other than that leave them to Queen Elizabeth. And doesn't SHE look nice?

Fashion Tips For Full Figured People.

1. Buy bigger clothes. If the indention of your belly button can be seen through your shirt, then your clothes are too tight. And if your clothes are tight you only look fatter than you really are and trust me, you don't need

the help. Loose fitting clothes make you look smaller.

2. Pull your pants up to the middle of your waist. If you wear your pants below your belly you only look fatter. Your pants should hit you in the middle of your stomach.

3. Think monochromatic. Don't break your body into sections, especially top half/bottom half. Guys, that means you should probably dump your white shirts and buy darker shirts closer to the color of your pants or suit. Women, the same applies to you, and make sure that your hose are darker too – otherwise your legs will look heavy.

4. Steer clear of knit. That means t-shirts, sweaters, knit skirts, etc. And don't wear a turtleneck, you will look like a huge turtle.

5. Wear tops that can be worn out and not tucked in. They lengthen your look and make you look slimmer.

6. Don't decorate it. You know what I mean. Big people should tone it down and not

accentuate. Plaid and gaudy prints are not your friends.

A Rule To Remember:

The less skin you have
the more of it you can show.
And if you have a lot of skin,
don't let us see it.

To Make More Sales

just do this stuff:

1. Talk to one more person every day. That will give you over two hundred more contacts per year. At your current closing rate, how much more money would that be worth to you?

2. Smile more and have a terrific handshake.

3. Master the first two minutes. Get great at introducing yourself and explaining what you do and what you want. You don't have long before the decision to buy or pass is made, so get good quick.

4. Ask for referrals.

5. Study selling. There are lots of great books out there. Read them.

6. Become very familiar with the problem your product solves. When you understand the problem, you'll be better at representing the solution.

7. Discover how your product or service serves other people. Commit to serving as many people as possible. The more you focus on serving others, the greater your rewards will be.

8. Ask for the sale. Every time. Never leave any selling situation without asking the customer to buy. Always!

9. Say thank you.

10. Do what you say you are going to do.

11. Do more than you say you are going to do.

12. Tell the truth. Period. No matter what. Even if it keeps you from making the sale.

13. Be great on the telephone.

14. Look good and smell good.

15. Develop a positive expectancy of success.

16. Know when to walk away. It's usually quicker than you think.

17. Have lots of stuff going.

18. Become the kind of person that other people enjoy doing business with.

19. Remember that it is impossible to lose a sale. You cannot lose what you never had to begin with.

20. Never be late. No reason is a good enough reason to be late.

21. Remember that it is better to under-promise and over-perform than it is to over-promise and under-perform.

22. Forget the word "competition." It just doesn't matter. Focus only on how you are unique and become committed to serving other through your uniqueness.

Discover your

and learn to exploit it in the service of others and you are guaranteed success, happiness, and prosperity.

To Be Healthy

just do this stuff:

1. Read labels. Cut down on fat, salt, calories, and things with names you can't pronounce.

2. Exercise regularly.

3. Take ten deep breathes at least three times per day.

4. Eat less.

5. Do what you love.

6. Play more.

7. Study health.

8. Walk.

9. Don't smoke.

10. Drink only in moderation.

11. Think health. Expect health. Speak only in terms of health.

12. Practice prevention.

13. Learn about herbs and use them to improve your immune system. Why have to get well when it is possible to stay healthy?

14. Only go to a healthy doctor. Stay away from overweight doctors who smoke.

15. Decide never to be victimized by illness. Refuse to participate.

To Be A Better Person

just do this stuff:

1. Surround yourself with the kind of people you would like to be.

2. Read good books.

3. Listen to good stuff. Fill your mind with the pure, the powerful, the positive and the prosperous.

4. Set goals for every area of your life.

5. Think in terms of your blessings instead of your limitations.

6. Forget blame.

7. Abandon judgment in all forms.

8. Speak only in positive terms. This applies to yourself, other people, and all conditions.

9. Be reliable, flexible, punctual, available and decisive.

10. Be a good listener.

To Be Smarter

just do this stuff:

1. Set aside thirty minutes per day to read. Offer yourself no excuses. Anyone can find thirty minutes. Start by turning off the television.

2. Only read things that make you better. Hint. Find out what poor people are reading, then don't read that. Start with the best sellers in the areas of self-help and business. If you still don't have a clue, go out and buy *The Greatest Salesman In The World* by Og Mandino. There is no better place to start.

Or call me, I highly recommend all of my books.

(The newspaper does not count. Your thirty minutes should be spent reading only the positive.)

3. Buy self-help audio tapes and listen to them in your car. Top-forty radio will not make you a better parent, spouse, or business person. Turn off the radio and turn on the tapes.

4. Hang around smart people. Ask good questions. Listen. Take notes.

To Give Better Customer Service

just do this stuff:

1. Be flexible.

2. Be friendly.

3. Take notes. Always work from document, not from memory.

4. When *anyone* makes a mistake, say that you are sorry.

5. Take responsibility for everything. Never lay blame elsewhere.

6. Everything that effects the customer is important. Act like it.

7. Do exactly what you say you are going to do, when you say you are going to, the way you said you were going to do it.

8. Follow up to assure satisfaction.

9. Find out what the customer wants and do your dead-level best to give it to them.

10. Do more than you have to and more than is expected.

To Cook 5 Great Meals

just do this stuff:

Everyone should be able to cook at least a couple of good things. You really only need about four or five good recipes to impress people (if they come to your house more often than that, then move). So here are my best recipes. These are so simple and anyone can look like a hero!

Corn Chowder

1 cup chopped onion
1/2 cup chopped celery
2 tablespoons butter or margarine
3 cups fresh corn
    (yeah right, buy a bag of frozen corn)
2 chopped carrots
1 1/2 cups cubed potatoes
    (peeled or unpeeled your preference)
1 1/2 cups water
2 chicken flavored bouillon cubes
1 teaspoon salt
    (use as much as you like)
1 teaspoon pepper
    (use as much as you like but I like more than this)
1/4 teaspoon dried whole thyme
2 cups half-and-half

Sauté onion and celery in butter in a large saucepan until tender. Stir in the rest of the ingredients except for the half-and-half; cover and simmer for about 15 minutes. Add half-and-half; cook, stirring constantly, until thoroughly heated. You can add a little flour to thicken if you like.

Yield 8 cups.

Dill Salmon

2 lemons
4 salmon steaks, 8 oz. each
3 tablespoons fresh dill, chopped
(use the bottled stuff if you have to)
3 tablespoons fresh thyme
(use the bottle stuff here too if you need to)
4 tablespoons unsalted butter

1. Grate the lemon peels for the 2 lemons into lemon zest.

2. Wipe the salmon steaks with damp paper towels, and then sprinkle both sides with dill, thyme and lemon zest.

3. Cut four 12 inch squares of aluminum foil and place one salmon steak on the lower half of each square. Top each steak with 1 tablespoon of butter.

4. Bring the top half of the foil over to form a rectangle and crimp the edges to seal.

5. When the grill is hot, place the packets on the grill and cook for 4 minutes, then turn them over and cook for 4 minutes on the other side.

6. Open the packets and serve.

Chicken Festiva ala Larry

Boneless chicken breasts
    (as many as you have people)
One small purple onion
One avocado
One green bell pepper
One red bell pepper
One yellow bell pepper
One tomato
A bottle of wine – anything you plan on drinking – red
    or white – it doesn't matter
Grated Monterrey jack and cheddar cheese
Salt and pepper

Use the biggest plumpest boneless chicken breasts you can find. Place a chicken breast in the middle of a 12-inch square of aluminum foil. Wedge avocado, red bell pepper, yellow bell pepper and green bell pepper, a small wedge of purple onion and a wedge of tomato. Alternate each of the above across the top of the breast to make it colorful. Then salt and pepper lightly. Then fold the edges of the aluminum foil up to make a sort of boat out of it so it will hold a shot of wine. Pour in the wine and seal the foil. Place the packets on the grill and cook until done. How long depends on the size and thickness of the chicken breast and how hot your fire is, usually about 20 minutes. When done, open the foil and cover with grated cheese and then leave on the grill until the cheese is melted. Carefully remove from the foil and place on the plate with the vegetables still on the top.

Larry's Southwest Soup

This is the easiest thing you will ever make. Any idiot can do this in about 20 minutes and be a hero.

2 Chicken Breasts
One small onion, chopped
One clove garlic, chopped
One-fourth cup chopped cilantro
(or as much as you want)
One cup frozen corn
(or a can of corn will work)
One can pinto beans
One can black beans
One small can green salsa verde
One can chopped tomatoes
One can chopped green chiles
One packet taco seasoning
Pepper to taste

Boil the chicken breasts in water. When done remove the breasts and cube. Skim as much of the fat as you can from the remaining broth in the saucepan. Brown the onion and garlic in a small pan and then dump all of the stuff in the pan and add water if needed. Simmer for about 20 minutes.

Larry's Killer Alfredo Sauce

Heat a small amount of olive oil in a good-sized saucepan. Sauté mushrooms, chopped onion and garlic until onions are clear and mushrooms are soft. (The quantities used are up to you and based on how much of this wonderful stuff you want in your Alfredo sauce.) Add a generous half-cup of white wine to the sauce pan and reduce it by half. Add 2 cups of whipping cream and reduce it by about a third. Salt and pepper to taste. Pour this over fettuccine pasta and dig in. This stuff is high fat, high calorie and highly delicious.

To Get More Done

just do this stuff:

1. Focus on accomplishment, not activity.
2. Have a written plan of what must be done.
3. Refuse to become involved in any thing that does not move you closer to the accomplishment of your goals.
4. Become stingy with your time.
5. Get really good at saying no.

6. Beware of meetings.

7. Complete one thing before beginning another.

8. Beware of the telephone. Don't let it interrupt what must be done.

9. Shut your door.

10. Work when other people are not around: during lunch hours, before others come in and after they go home.

11. To get more done at home:

    a. Stand up more. You get very little done when sitting on your rear. (I do approve of sitting down to read, though.)

    b. Turn off the television.

To Forgive Others

just do this stuff:

1. Make a list of everyone you feel has wronged you. Write down every name that comes to mind regardless of how insignificant it may seem.

2. Be sure to include your own name. You will forgive others to the same extent that you forgive yourself.

3. Go down the list working through the pain of each wrong. Don't re-live the wrong. Move through the pain to a point of healing.

Release the power that these people and situations hold over you. Take all the time you need. As you are able to forgive, mark the name off the list and move on to the next name.

4. If you feel that you must contact the person involved, think long and hard about it. It may not be in everyone's best interest to open up old wounds. Forgiving is a personal process that involves you more than it does anyone else.

5. If you absolutely feel that you must contact them, then be cautious. They may not remember the thing at all, or may have moved past it long ago.

6. Forgiveness works two ways. If you feel the need to ask forgiveness, approach the other person cautiously. They may have forgotten it or have no idea what you are talking about.

7. Know that forgiveness is a necessary step for being successful and achieving prosperity.

8. Try reaching the point where you understand that nobody actually ever did you any wrong to begin with. Everything that has happened to you has caused you to become more. Becoming more is always a good thing.

What I think about, talk about, and do something about, comes about.

©Larry Winget, 800 749-4597

To Be More Thankful

just do this stuff:

1. Make a "thankful for" list. List things like your house, your car, your friends, your abilities, your stuff, your family, your knowledge, your health, and your job. List the little things, too.

2. Know that regardless of how little you may feel you have to be thankful for, it could always be worse!

3. Begin every single day by writing down at least five things you are thankful for.

4. Remember that everything that happens to you causes you to grow in some way, even the lousy stuff. Be thankful for everything.

5. Remember the people who *really* have it bad. By comparison, you probably have it pretty good. (By the way, as long as you are thinking of those folks who really have it bad, why not think of some way to help them?)

To Be A Better Manager/Leader

just do this stuff:

1. People are everything. Act like it.

2. Study. There are probably more books written on this subject than any other. Buy them. Read them.

3. Be proactive. You set the pace. No one will be any better or worse than you are. As the example, be and do your best.

4. Have very high expectations. People will normally live up to or down to what you expect from them.

5. Become a great communicator.

6. Ask lots of questions. Then listen.

7. Let everyone know exactly what you expect from them.

8. Manage and lead from the workplace, not from your desk.

9. Be flexible.

10. Everyone is different. Treat them that way.

11. Teach people what you want them to know.

12. Don't assume anything.

13. Say thank you more than you think you should. People want your appreciation more than just about anything else.

14. Give constant feedback.

15. Never accept mediocrity.

16. Lavish praise privately and publicly.

17. Critique performance privately. Notice that says *performance*. That's the only thing you have the right to critique.

18. Forget constructive criticism. Constructive means to build up and criticism means to tear down. It is impossible to do both at the same time.

19. Stop spending your time putting out fires. Instead:

    a. Teach your people not to start fires.

    b. Teach them to put out their own fires.

    c. If this doesn't work, get new people.

20. Measure two things: willingness and ability. Those without ability need training. Those without willingness need to work somewhere else.

21. Have fun and help others have fun.

To Manage Stress

just do this stuff:

1. Stop trying to manage your stress. Why would you want to manage something that you don't want any way?

2. Determine what causes stress. This is what I have learned about stress:

   Stress comes from
   knowing what is right and
   doing what is wrong.

3. Be willing to do what is right.

4. Stay scoped up.

5. Learn how to meditate.

6. Exercise.

7. Stop worrying about what might happen. It rarely happens anyway so why worry about it?

8. Give up having to have control over every detail of your life. Learn to trust the Universe.

To Delegate

just do this stuff:

1. Ask yourself these questions:

   a. Can it be done faster by someone else?

   b. Can it be done better by someone else?

   c. Can it be done cheaper by someone else?

   d. Can it be done by someone who enjoys it more?

2. If the answer if yes to any of these questions, then delegate.

3. Give up all emotional ties to the task. It is not important who does it, only that it gets done.

4. Never worry about taking credit, only about giving credit.

5. Ask other people for their help. People love to help when they are asked. People don't love being told what to do.

6. Explain clearly exactly what is expected and when.

7. Say thank you.

To Travel Better On Airplanes

just do this stuff:

Because of the business I am in, I spend more time on airplanes than most folks do. I have reached the highest level in most all the frequent flyer programs on most airlines. And don't think that being a frequent flyer entitles you to any real privileges. The only thing being at that highest, most privileged level does for you is get you on the plane earlier so you can be mistreated longer.

Not long ago I was sitting in the bulkhead seat in first class with my feet on the carpeted wall in front of me. The flight attendant shook her head at me disapprovingly and said "If you were at home would your wife let you put your feet on the wall like that?" I told her "If I had to pay her $700 and hour to sit there, she would."

And after having flown many million miles this list makes up most of what I have learned about flying and includes what ticks me off.

1. When you walk down the aisle, put your carry on bags in front of you so you don't bang people in the head.

2. Regarding carry on bags: they've got this box to stick your bag in to make sure it will fit in the overhead compartment. If there is a question in your mind, then use the box. Get a clue about how big your bag is. Don't get on the plane with dozens of people behind you and then start trying to figure out how to make that big bag squish in that little bitty place.

3. Remember that the seat table in front of you is on the back of someone else's chair. Don't pound on it and don't let your little kid pound on it either.

4. Don't pass gas. Don't sneeze without your hand covering your honker. Don't cough without covering your mouth. While these are important things to remember regardless of where you are, it is especially important on airplanes because there is a limited amount of space and air: odors and germs travel faster and don't have anywhere to go.

5. Don't feel compelled to talk to your seat mate. In other words, don't speak until spoken to. Sound harsh? Some people really just don't want to talk. It is not that they are unfriendly, it is just that they don't want to talk. In my case, it is because when I get on an airplane I want to rest. I travel all the time and I want to use the flight time to rest and read.

6. Don't sit in the boarding area (or the bar) until they announce the final boarding call and then rush to get on the plane before they shut the door and then open every overhead compartment looking for a place to put your oversized bag. There IS no place. You got there too late. Don't complain, don't ask for

help, and don't mutter under your breath. It's your own fault – sit down and kick and push and smash that thing up under the seat in front of you and next time get on the plane when they call your row number.

7. Don't sigh loudly or moan and say things like "Oh what a day!" in order to get attention. Personally, I won't take the bait. I won't talk to you. I promise.

One time, I actually had someone reach over and pull the headset off of my ear to say, "Hi! Having a good day?" Answer: "I was until you did that." I also had someone wake me up to ask, "If you died on this plane crash do you know if you would end up in heaven or hell?" I decided this question was a sure-fire conversation killer. In fact, those two experiences spurred me into action and I actually designed and printed some book covers to guarantee that no one will talk to me on airplanes.

How To Sue
The Person In The Seat Next To You
On An Airplane
by
LARRY WINGET

How to SELL INSURANCE
To People On Airplanes
by
LARRY WINGET

THE COMPLETE
Ambulance Chaser's Guide
To Airline Travel
by
LARRY WINGET

FINDING
LOVE
ON AN
AIRPLANE
"I'm from Mars, you're from Venus, let's get together and explore Uranus!"

The Big Questions of Life
Am I happy?
Am I healthy?
Am I serving?
Am I loving?
Am I learning?
Am I having fun?
Am I doing something I enjoy?
Am I prosperous?
If the answer to all of these questions is yes, then celebrate.
If the answer to any of these questions is no, then do something immediately to change things.
www.larrywinget.com

To Reward People

just do this stuff:

1. Do it immediately.

2. Tie the reward to very specific behavior. The more specific, the stronger the impact.

3. Be creative with your rewards. Money is old news; so are plaques, and trophies. Use your imagination.

4. Keep your rewards positive.

5. Do it verbally. Say thank you and I appreciate you.

6. Do it non-verbally. Write a note. Again, be specific and positive.

7. Do it often.

To Be More Enthusiastic

just do this stuff:

1. Hang around enthusiastic people. Enthusiasm is contagious.

2. Start every day by thinking enthusiastically. The way you begin your day sets the mood for the entire day.

3. Become acutely aware of the good stuff going on in the world around you. And there really is lots of good going on regardless of what others would have you believe.

4. Give your enthusiasm away. Let people see and feel the passion you have for life. What you give away comes back to you. Give your enthusiasm away and you will find a never ending reservoir to draw upon.

5. Run from the gripers, whiners, moaners and groaners!

6. Practice. Practice. Practice.

To Deal With A Jerk

just do this stuff:

1. Remember that sometimes you are a jerk, too. This will help you keep it in perspective.

2. You can't change the way people are, you can only change the way you respond to them. So why drive yourself crazy? Lighten up.

3. Know that it's rarely personal.

4. Forgive them, they can't help it. Most jerks have received years of training in order to get good at it.

5. Be more understanding. Maybe they are just having a bad day.

6. Don't give them the power to ruin your day. They're jerks, remember? Why would you want to put a jerk in charge?

7. Be nice. Jerks hate that and will sometimes stop being one just to spite you.

8. Know that people aren't really jerks. They just act in jerky ways.

To Be More Positive

just do this stuff:

1. Stop whining and griping.
2. Remember that it could always be worse.
3. Speak and think in terms of what you can do instead of what you can't.
4. Surround yourself with positive people.
5. Read and listen to positive stuff.
6. Don't watch too much TV news, or listen to the radio news or read the newspaper.

Believe me, you will still find out the important stuff.

7. Look for the good in every situation.

8. Recall the most used line in the Bible, "And it came to pass." That's good news. It didn't come to stay!

9. Focus on others instead of yourself.

10. Stop being negative.

To Manage Your Time Better

just do this stuff:

1. Use the trash can more often. Throw away more stuff. You are probably saving and filing way too many things.

2. Handle every piece of paper only once.

3. End every day by preparing a list of what must get done tomorrow.

4. Throw your To Do lists away. You have plenty to do without putting it on a list.

5. Get a To Get Done list. Concentrate on what you must get done instead of what you need to do. Focus on accomplishment instead of activity.

6. Have a clean desk and only work on one thing at a time.

7. Always keep a pen and paper handy.

8. Get a junk drawer. If you have any question about whether something is going to be useful, then put it in the drawer. About once a month, dump the drawer. If you can do without the stuff for a month, then it wasn't worthwhile to begin with.

9. Collect all of your junk mail for thirty days. At the end of the thirty days, contact each company and ask that your name be removed from their mailing list. Not only is your time saved, but you have had a positive impact on every person who touched that piece of mail.

10. Set aside a specific time for returning telephone calls and then really return your calls.

To Be Happier

just do this stuff:

1. Give up the need to be right. You can choose: do you want to be right or happy?
2. Scope up – give up pettiness at all levels.
3. Be healthy. It's hard to be happy when you are sick or don't feel well.
4. Be more loving.
5. Serve others well.
6. Stop being so judgmental.

7. Compliment others. You will be happier than you have made them.
8. Continue to learn. A challenged mind is happier than a bored one.
9. Be involved.
10. Know who you are.
11. Be who you are.
12. Enjoy who you are.
13. Rise above the approval of others.
14. Do things that you enjoy.
15. Learn how to relax.
16. Remember that failure is temporary and is not an indication of your worth and what you can ultimately accomplish.
17. Master the ability to forgive.
18. Learn to enjoy your money.
19. Be generous.

20. Learn to be satisfied with what you have while you are on your way to getting more.

21. Begin to trust more. The Universe WANTS you to win.

22. Don't get your panties in a wad. In the long run, none of this really matters anyway.

Shut Up™
Stop Whining
AND GET A
LIFE!

To Be Better On The Telephone

just do this stuff:

1. Always have a pen and paper by your telephone. Nothing is dumber or more rude than to ask people to wait while you get prepared.

2. Get a long cord. You are better when you have the ability to stand up and move around.

3. Slow down when you answer. Make sure that the caller can actually understand who is answering.

4. Stay focused.

5. When calling anyone, introduce yourself first. Don't make them have to ask who is calling.

6. Always leave your number. Don't force the other person to scrounge around looking for it.

7. Be careful about leaving messages. Most people don't return their calls in a timely manner, if at all. If it is an important call, then you be the one who calls back.

8. Don't leave people on hold for more than thirty seconds. People can't see what you are doing and will think you went to the bathroom.

9. Answer on the second ring. If you answer on the first, they will assume that you don't have anything else to do. If you answer on the third, fourth, or more, then they will assume that you are goofing off.

10. Summarize the call and confirm understanding before you hang up. This saves unnecessary callbacks and keeps both of you from looking stupid because someone forgot something.

To Run Better Meetings

just do this stuff:

1. Start on time.
2. Have an agenda. No agenda, no meeting.
3. Only involve people who are essential to the decision. The fewer, the better.
4. Stay focused. If it is not critical to the matter at hand, then discuss it later.
5. Less food, more content. Donuts are not an essential ingredient for conducting an effective meeting.

6. Keep it short. Business meetings that last more than an hour are too long.

7. Be prepared. Never come to a meeting without being fully prepared.

8. Stop on time.

9. Encourage everyone to take notes.

10. Do everything within your power to keep from having a meeting. If it can be handled with a memo or a phone call, then by all means, do it.

To Be A Better Friend And Have More Friends

just do this stuff:

1. Make a list of the qualities describing the kind of friend you would like to have.

2. Become the person on the list.

3. Tell your friends how much you appreciate them and why.

4. Be a good listener.

5. Never tell someone something for their own good. They don't want to hear it. Besides, it's not really for their own good; it's for yours.

6. Honesty is the best policy.

7. Remember that true friendship is unconditional.

8. When you mess up (and you will) be quick to apologize. Friends are hard to come by, so do everything you can to hang on to one.

9. Be quick to forgive.

10. Only have friends who encourage you to be more, do more, and have more. A friend who discourages you in any way is not your friend . . . dump them quick!

To Deal More Effectively With Change

just do this stuff:

1. Be flexible. Remember that change is ALWAYS about process. Process is HOW you do your job. How you do your job will change. It has to. Change is not about purpose. Purpose is WHY you do your job. Why you do your job will never change. You do your job for one reason and one reason only and that is to serve others well. Be inflexible with purpose (why you do your job). Be flexible with process (how you do your job).

2. Accept change – it is here to stay.
3. Enjoy change. Learn to look forward to what is going to happen next.
4. Become more valuable to your organization. This is great insurance for your future. The most valued always have a job.
5. Stay positive in your outlook about what is going on.
6. Get current and stay that way. Don't let new technology, ideas, books, systems, etc. pass you by. Stay up to date by taking classes and reading. Keep learning.
7. Expect the best. What you expect is what you usually get.
8. Look for the good. Every change brings with it some good points. Find them and enjoy them.
9. Scope up. Don't be petty.
10. Don't become emotionally attached to any policy, procedure, style, technique, boss or co-worker.

To Make Better Business Presentations

just do this stuff:

1. Know the message you would like to have your audience leave with. Make sure they leave with it.

2. Establish and maintain eye contact. Look at the friendly faces in the crowd.

3. Be natural. You can only be yourself anyway, so enjoy it.

4. Take some deep breaths before going on.

5. Picture yourself doing well. (Your audience really does want you to do well and will help you if you will give them a chance.)

6. Humor is always appropriate. That doesn't mean that you have to be a stand-up comic. It just means that everyone will enjoy your presentation more and will retain the information better if they have enjoyed themselves.

7. Have a strong opening and a strong finish. Your audience will forgive you for most of what goes on in between.

8. Never admit that you are anything but prepared, confident, and ready. Chances are they will never know the difference. And if you really aren't, why are you there to begin with?

9. Move around, but don't pace.

10. Visuals should be uncluttered and extremely simple.

11. Never put down anyone in your audience for any reason.

12. Use gestures. Make them appropriate to the point you are making.

13. Accept that you will make mistakes. Big deal. People rarely die from making speeches.

14. Involve your audience by assigning a mental task to perform, by having them raise their hands, by making them move around, by using names, or by asking them to write down something you just said or are about to say.

15. Style is important. Get some.

16. Facial expressions are important. Have one.

17. Practice.

18. Believe what you have to say. People will pay very little attention to what you have to say. Most won't even believe what you have to say. However, they will pay attention to see if *you* believe what you have to say.

19. Finish on time, regardless of when you went on. People become hostile when they are held past the expected time.

We enter life like a question mark, full of wonder and curiosity — and we leave it like a period as if we have all the answers.
If you have to live your life like a punctuation mark, live it like an exclamation point!
www.larrywinget.com

To Deal More Effectively With Problems

just do this stuff:

1. Know that problems are a normal occurrence and happen to everyone.

2. Understand that problems cause you to grow. Anything that causes you to grow is a good thing.

3. Look beyond the problem.

4. Break the problem down into small pieces and deal with the pieces.

5. Stop disasterizing the problem. The worst that could happen rarely happens.

6. Write the problem down. Somehow when you look at it in black and white, it just doesn't seem so overwhelming.

7. Focus on the solution.

8. Get help. Find someone who knows more than you do about solving the problem, and ask for their help.

To Have A Better Life

just do this stuff:

Larry's Fast Track Plan For A Better Life

1. Decide what you want.

2. Know that you deserve it.

3. Believe that you can have it.

4. Focus your energy toward it.

5. Do something toward making it happen.

6. Keep doing more until it happens.

7. Enjoy yourself while making it happen.

8. Be thankful regardless of what happens.

To Be A Better Communicator

just do this stuff:

1. Be a good listener.

2. Establish and maintain eye contact.

3. Ask lots of questions.

4. Give good feedback. Nod your head and say stuff that lets them know you are paying attention.

5. Act like what the other person is saying is the most interesting thing you ever heard.

6. You are always responsible for any communications. If anyone drops the ball, it is your job to pick it up.

7. Don't interrupt.

8. Become comfortable with silence.

9. Sincerely believe what you say. If you don't, then just keep quiet.

10. Be proactive, not reactive.

To Make A Better World

just do this stuff:

1. Love.
2. Recycle.
3. Abandon judgement in all forms.
4. Support organizations who feed and clothe those who need it.
5. Take care of the earth.
6. Don't litter.

7. Be for things instead of against things.

8. Make at least one other person smile every day.

9. Don't talk in movie theaters.

10. Never smack your gum.

Short Lists

❶

just do this stuff:

- **To get started**

  Just start.

- **To quit smoking**

  Don't put cigarettes in your mouth.

- **To deal with criticism**

  Don't. Rise above the approval of others.

- **To deal with guilt.**

  Forget guilt. It serves no purpose. You can't change one thing that ever happened. Forgive yourself; ask for forgiveness if you need to, learn from the experience, act differently in the future and move on.

- **To deal with an idiot.**

  Don't. They're idiots.

Is that all there is?

Of course not. These lists are not the end-all, be-all, do-all for success in every area of your life. I never intended them to be.

There is a lot more than this. But chances are very good that most people will never look for it or do it. It's just too much effort.

So, this is definitely not all there is. However, it is most of what you need in order to have much better results than you are currently experiencing.

If you will just do the stuff on these lists, then you will become more successful than you have been. The more successful you become, the more you will seek to find bigger and even more profound ideas. So these lists are great beginnings for everyone and very good endings for most.

Regardless of the path you decide to follow, remember the premise of this entire book:

It's not hard!

Success comes from doing just a few things that most people don't or won't do.

I leave you with one of my favorite quotes:

After all is said and done,
more is said than done.

. . . Unknown

Now go out and do something!

Larry Winget, CSP

Larry Winget is a philosopher of success who just happens to be hilarious. He teaches universal principles that will work for anyone, in any business, at any time, and does it by telling funny stories. He believes that most of us have complicated life and business way too much, take it way too seriously and that we need to lighten up, take respon-sibility, be more flexible, stay positive and keep it in perspective. He believes that success and prosperity come from serving others. He teaches that business improves when the people in the business improve and that everything in life gets better when we get better and nothing gets better until we get better.

To have Larry speak to your organization or to order any of his other personal and professional development products, please go to:

www.larrywinget.com

For a complete catalog of Larry Winget's books, audio and video learning systems, and other unique personal development products, contact:

Win Seminars! Inc.
P. O. Box 700485
Tulsa, Oklahoma 74170
918 745-6606
800 749-4597

Or go to:
www.larrywinget.com